GOOGLE FORMS

FOR BEGINNERS

The Complete Step-By-Step Guide To Creating And Sharing Online Forms And Surveys, And Analyzing Responses In Real-time

GOOGLE FORMS FOR BEGINNERS

The Complete Step-By-Step Guide To Creating And Sharing Online Forms And Surveys, And Analyzing Responses In Real-time

While every precaution has been taken in the preparation of this book, the publisher assumes no responsibility for errors or omissions, or for damages resulting from the use of the information contained herein.

GOOGLE FORMS FOR BEGINNERS: THE COMPLETE STEP-BY-STEP GUIDE TO CREATING AND SHARING ONLINE FORMS AND SURVEYS, AND ANALYZING RESPONSES IN REAL-TIME

First edition. November 27, 2023.

Copyright © 2023 Voltaire Lumiere.

Written by Voltaire Lumiere.

TABLE OF CONTENTS

CHAPTER 1

INTRODUCTION TO GOOGLE FORMS

- **What are Online Forms and Surveys?**

Online forms and surveys have become integral tools for gathering information, feedback, and insights in the digital age. These electronic counterparts to traditional paper forms offer a dynamic and efficient means of collecting data from individuals across the globe.

Online forms are digital documents created to capture user input, typically through a series of fields or questions. They range from simple feedback forms and contact forms to complex surveys and registration forms. These forms are accessible through web browsers, making them convenient for both creators and respondents.

Surveys, a specific type of online form, are structured sets of questions designed to gather specific information or opinions from a targeted audience. Surveys are widely used in various fields, including market research, academic studies, and organizational assessments. They provide a structured framework for obtaining quantitative and qualitative data, enabling a systematic analysis of responses.

The shift from traditional paper forms to online counterparts brings numerous advantages. Online forms and surveys offer a faster and more cost-effective means of data collection, eliminating the need for physical distribution and manual data entry. The digital nature of these tools allows for real-time data capture and analysis, providing immediate insights into trends and patterns.

Furthermore, the flexibility of online forms enables customization to suit specific needs. Creators can easily incorporate various question types, including multiple-choice, open-ended, and rating scales. This adaptability enhances the precision and depth of information collected, ensuring a comprehensive understanding of the subject matter.

In essence, online forms and surveys represent a dynamic and efficient evolution in data collection methods. Their accessibility, versatility, and real-time capabilities make them invaluable tools for individuals, businesses, and researchers seeking to gather accurate and timely information in today's interconnected world.

- **The Power of Google Forms**

The power of Google Forms lies in its seamless integration into the Google Workspace ecosystem and its user-friendly features that simplify the process of creating, distributing, and analyzing forms and surveys.

At its core, Google Forms provides a free and accessible platform for users to design customized forms without the need for advanced technical skills. Its intuitive interface allows creators to effortlessly add various types of questions, including multiple-choice, short answer, and dropdowns. This versatility caters to a wide range of data collection needs, from simple feedback forms to complex research surveys.

One of the standout features is the real-time collaboration enabled by Google Forms. Multiple users can collaborate simultaneously on form creation, making it an ideal tool for teams working on projects or events. The seamless integration with other Google Workspace apps, such as Google Sheets, further streamlines the data collection and analysis process.

The ability to collect responses in real-time enhances the immediacy of insights. As respondents submit their answers, creators can instantly view and analyze the data within the Google Forms interface. The integration with Google Sheets facilitates the automatic transfer of responses, allowing for in-depth data manipulation and visualization.

Google Forms also excels in its accessibility and distribution options. Forms can be easily shared via a link, embedded on websites, or sent directly through email. The simplicity of these distribution methods ensures a broad reach and encourages higher response rates.

Furthermore, the platform's responsive design ensures a seamless experience for both creators and respondents across various devices, including desktops, tablets, and mobile phones. This adaptability enhances the accessibility of forms, making it convenient for users to participate from anywhere.

In summary, the power of Google Forms lies in its user-friendly design, real-time collaboration capabilities, seamless integration with other Google Workspace apps, and accessibility across devices. Whether used for simple data collection or extensive research projects, Google Forms empowers users to efficiently gather, analyze, and derive valuable insights from their collected data.

- **Setting Up Your Google Forms Account**

Setting up your Google Forms account is a straightforward process that grants you access to a versatile platform for creating, sharing, and analyzing forms and surveys. Here's a brief guide to get you started:

1. **Google Account Creation:**

- To begin, you need a Google Account. If you don't have one, you can easily create it by visiting the Google Account creation page.

- Provide the necessary information, including a valid email address and a secure password.

2. **Accessing Google Forms:**

• Once your Google Account is set up, navigate to Google Drive (drive.google.com).

• In the upper left corner, click on the "+ New" button.

• From the drop-down menu, select "More," and then click on "Google Forms."

3. **Google Forms Interface:**

• You are now in the Google Forms interface, where you can start creating your forms.

• Familiarize yourself with the toolbar at the top, which provides options for adding questions, changing the form settings, and more.

4. **Creating Your First Form:**

• Click on the "+ Blank" button to start a new form.

• Give your form a title by clicking on "Untitled form" in the top-left corner and entering a descriptive name.

5. **Adding Questions:**

• Use the various question types available (multiple-choice, short answer, etc.) to structure your form.

• Click on the "+" button to add a new question, and customize it based on your data collection needs.

6. **Form Settings:**

- Explore the settings icon (gear symbol) to customize your form further. Adjust settings such as confirmation messages, response collection limits, and more.

7. **Saving Your Form:**

- Google Forms automatically saves your work as you make changes. However, it's a good practice to click on the floppy disk icon (Save) to ensure your progress is saved.

8. **Accessing Saved Forms:**

- All your forms are stored in Google Drive. You can access them by returning to Google Drive and locating the "Forms" section in the left sidebar.

Congratulations! You've successfully set up your Google Forms account and created your first form. From here, you can continue to explore the platform's features, customize your forms, and efficiently collect and analyze data for various purposes.

- **Navigating the Google Forms Interface**

Navigating the Google Forms interface is essential for efficiently creating, editing, and managing your forms. Here's a guide to help you seamlessly move through the platform:

1. **Form Dashboard:**

- Upon entering Google Forms, you'll find yourself in the Form Dashboard. Here, you can view and access your existing forms or create a new one by clicking on the "+" icon.

2. **Form Editor:**

- Clicking on a form or creating a new one takes you to the Form Editor. This is where the magic happens.

- The toolbar at the top offers options to add questions, customize form settings, preview the form, and more.

3. **Form Title:**

- In the top-left corner, you'll find the form title. Click on it to rename your form and provide a clear, descriptive title.

4. **Add Questions:**

- Use the "+" button on the right side of the screen to add questions. This opens a menu with various question types. Choose the one that fits your data collection needs.

5. **Question Settings:**

- Once you've added a question, clicking on it reveals additional settings. Customize options like required status, answer validation, and more.

6. **Form Settings:**

- The gear icon in the top-right corner opens the Form Settings menu. Here, you can modify general settings such as collecting email addresses, limiting responses, and customizing confirmation messages.

7. **Preview:**

- Before finalizing your form, click the eye icon (Preview) to see how it will appear to respondents. This helps you ensure a user-friendly experience.

8. **Sidebar Navigation:**

- On the right side, you'll find the sidebar navigation. This allows you to easily switch between different sections of your form, such as Questions, Responses, and the Form Settings.

9. **Themes and Colors:**

- The paint palette icon lets you customize the theme and colors of your form. Experiment with different styles to make your form visually appealing.

10. **Form Options:**

- The three dots in the top-right corner open a menu with additional options. Here, you can duplicate the form, print it, or explore add-ons for extended functionality.

11. **Real-time Collaboration:**

• Google Forms allows real-time collaboration. If you're working on a form with others, you can see their edits in real-time, enhancing teamwork.

Navigating the Google Forms interface is all about leveraging these tools to create a well-designed, effective form. As you become more familiar with the platform, you'll find that the intuitive layout and accessible features contribute to a seamless form creation experience.

• **Overview of Basic Features**

Google Forms comes packed with a range of basic features that make form creation and data collection straightforward. Here's an overview of these fundamental functionalities:

1. **Question Types:**

• Google Forms offers various question types, including multiple-choice, short answer, paragraph, and more. This versatility allows you to tailor your form to collect different types of information.

2. **Drag-and-Drop Interface:**

• The user-friendly drag-and-drop interface makes it easy to rearrange questions, sections, or even entire pages within your form. This flexibility ensures your form's structure suits your preferences.

3. Pre-built Templates:

*   If you're looking for inspiration or a quick start, Google Forms provides pre-built templates for common use cases. These templates cover surveys, event RSVPs, quizzes, and more.

4. Form Preview:

*   Before sharing your form, use the preview option to see how it will appear to respondents. This helps you catch any errors and ensures a smooth user experience.

5. Real-time Collaboration:

*   Google Forms supports real-time collaboration, allowing multiple users to work on the same form simultaneously. Edits and changes are visible to all collaborators instantly.

6. Form Settings:

*   Accessible through the gear icon, form settings let you customize various aspects. You can control who can respond, limit responses, shuffle question order, and even collect email addresses for respondent tracking.

7.   **Automatic Saving:**

•   Google Forms automatically saves your work as you create or edit a form. You can also manually save by clicking the floppy disk icon.

8.   **Response Collection:**

•   Responses are collected in real-time and stored in a linked Google Sheets spreadsheet. This spreadsheet provides a comprehensive view of all responses, making it easy to analyze and share data.

9.   **Share Options:**

•   Easily share your form using the share button. You can generate a link, send invitations via email, or embed the form on a website. This accessibility ensures a broad reach for your survey or data collection.

10.   **Mobile Responsiveness:**

•   Google Forms are designed to be mobile-responsive. Respondents can access and complete forms seamlessly on various devices, enhancing the user experience.

11.   **Data Validation:**

•   Customize questions with data validation rules to ensure respondents provide accurate and valid information. This feature helps maintain the integrity of your collected data.

12. **Add Images and Videos:**

• Enhance the visual appeal and clarity of your forms by easily adding images or embedding videos. This feature is particularly useful for instructional or descriptive purposes.

These basic features collectively contribute to Google Forms' accessibility, versatility, and efficiency in creating and managing online forms and surveys. Whether you're a beginner or an experienced user, these functionalities lay a solid foundation for a smooth form creation process.

CHAPTER 2

CREATING YOUR FIRST FORM

Starting a New Form

Creating a new form in Google Forms is a straightforward process. Here's a step-by-step guide on how to start a new form:

1. **Access Google Forms:**

*   Open your web browser and go to Google Drive by visiting drive.google.com.

2. **Sign In:**

*   If you're not already signed in, enter your Google Account credentials to log in. If you don't have a Google Account, you'll need to create one.

3. **Navigate to Google Forms:**

*   In Google Drive, click on the "+ New" button on the left side of the screen.

4. **Select "More" and then "Google Forms":**

*   A drop-down menu will appear when you click "+ New." Scroll down and select "More." From the expanded options, choose "Google Forms."

5. **Create a New Form:**

- Click on the "Google Forms" option to open the Forms dashboard. Here, you'll see a "+ Blank" template. Click on it to start a new form.

6. **Form Title:**

- In the top-left corner, you'll see "Untitled form." Click on it to give your form a title. Enter a descriptive name that reflects the purpose of your form.

7. **Adding Questions:**

- Use the "+" button on the right to add questions. You can choose from various question types such as multiple-choice, short answer, and more. Clicking on a question allows you to customize its settings.

8. **Form Toolbar:**

- Explore the toolbar at the top of the page for additional options. Here, you can customize the theme, preview your form, access form settings, and more.

9. **Automatic Saving:**

- Google Forms automatically saves your work as you make changes. You can also manually save by clicking on the floppy disk icon.

10. **Preview Your Form:**

- Before sharing your form, click the eye icon (Preview) to see how it will appear to respondents. This helps you ensure a user-friendly experience.

11. **Form URL:**

- Your form will have a unique URL. To find it, click on the "Send" button in the top-right corner. From here, you can copy the link to share with respondents.

12. **Collaborate in Real-time:**

- If you're working with others, you can collaborate in real-time. Simply share the form with collaborators using their email addresses, and you can all work on the form simultaneously.

Congratulations! You've successfully started a new form in Google Forms. From here, you can continue adding questions, custom

- **Adding and Editing Questions**

Adding and editing questions in Google Forms is a crucial step in tailoring your form to collect the information you need. Here's a detailed guide on how to add and edit questions:

Adding Questions:

1.   **Access the Form Editor:**

•   Open your Google Form and navigate to the Form Editor by clicking on the form title or selecting "Edit" when viewing the form.

2.   **Click the "+" Button:**

•   Inside the Form Editor, click on the "+" button on the right side of the screen. This opens the question menu.

3.   **Choose a Question Type:**

•   From the question menu, select the type of question you want to add. Options include multiple-choice, short answer, paragraph, and more.

4.   **Enter the Question:**

•   After selecting a question type, enter your question in the text box provided. You can also add any necessary instructions or context to guide respondents.

5.   **Customize Answer Options:**

•   For multiple-choice questions, add answer options by typing them into the fields provided. Google Forms allows you to add as many answer options as needed.

6. **Add Additional Questions:**

* To add more questions, click the "+" button again and repeat the process. You can mix different question types to create a comprehensive form.

Editing Questions:

1. **Click on the Question:**

* To edit an existing question, click directly on the question you want to modify. This action opens the question editor.

2. **Modify Question Text:**

* Edit the text of the question or any accompanying instructions. Ensure that the wording is clear and concise for respondents.

3. **Customize Answer Options:**

* For multiple-choice questions, you can add, edit, or delete answer options. Rearrange options by dragging them into the desired order.

4. **Question Settings:**

* Access additional question settings by clicking on the three dots next to a question. Here, you can mark a question as required, duplicate it, or delete it.

5.   **Logic and Branching:**

•   Explore the three dots menu for advanced options like adding logic and branching to questions. This feature allows you to show or skip questions based on specific responses.

6.   **Preview Your Changes:**

•   Before finalizing your form, click on the eye icon (Preview) to see how the changes appear to respondents. This helps you ensure the overall flow and clarity of your form.

7.   **Save Your Form:**

•   Google Forms automatically saves your work, but it's a good practice to click the floppy disk icon to manually save your changes.

By following these steps, you can efficiently add and edit questions in Google Forms, creating a well-structured and effective form for collecting responses.

•   **Types   of   Questions: Text, Multiple Choice, and More**

Google Forms offers a variety of question types to cater to different data collection needs. Here's an overview of some common question types you can use:

1. Text Questions:

- *Short Answer:* Respondents provide a brief text response. Useful for open-ended questions.

- *Paragraph:* Similar to short answer but allows for longer responses.

2. Multiple Choice:

- *Multiple Choice:* Respondents select one option from a list of choices.

- *Checkboxes:* Allows respondents to select multiple options from a list.

3. Dropdown:

- *Dropdown:* Presents a list of options in a dropdown menu. Saves space when you have a long list of choices.

4. File Upload:

- *File Upload:* Enables respondents to upload files. Useful for collecting documents or images.

5. Linear Scale:

- *Linear Scale:* Respondents rate an item on a scale. Useful for measuring satisfaction or agreement.

6. Multiple Choice Grid:

- *Multiple Choice Grid:* Allows respondents to select options for multiple statements in a grid format.

7. Checkbox Grid:

- *Checkbox Grid:* Similar to multiple choice grid but allows for multiple selections.

8. Date and Time:

- *Date:* Asks respondents to select a date from a calendar.

- *Time:* Asks respondents to enter a specific time.

9. Rating Scale:

- *Rating Scale:* Respondents rate an item on a numerical scale. Useful for measuring opinions or preferences.

10. Section Break:

- *Section Break:* Divides your form into sections. Useful for organizing and structuring longer forms.

11. Page Break:

- *Page Break:* Splits your form into multiple pages. Useful for creating a more organized and user-friendly survey experience.

12. Image and Video:

- *Image:* Allows you to insert an image into your form.

- *Video:* Embeds a video into your form. Useful for providing additional context or instructions.

13. Scale:

- *Scale:* Similar to linear scale but allows for a wider range of responses.

14. Yes/No:

- *Yes/No:* Requires a simple yes or no response.

15. Location:

- *Location:* Asks respondents to provide their current location.

These question types offer flexibility in designing surveys and forms tailored to your specific objectives. By strategically using different question types, you can gather a wide range of information efficiently and effectively.

- **Customizing Form Settings**

Customizing form settings in Google Forms allows you to control various aspects of the form-taking experience. Here's a guide on how to customize form settings:

1. Accessing Form Settings:

- While in the Form Editor, click on the gear icon in the top-right corner. This opens the Form Settings menu.

2. General Settings:

- In the General tab, you can:

- Change the form title by editing the "Form name."

- Provide a description for additional context.

- Choose to collect respondents' email addresses.

3. Presentation Settings:

- The Presentation tab allows you to:

- Shuffle the question order to minimize order bias.

- Show progress bar to respondents.

- Customize the "Submit" button text.

4. Quizzes Settings:

- If your form is a quiz, navigate to the Quizzes tab to:

- Enable quizzes by toggling on "Make this a quiz."

- Assign point values to questions.

- Choose when to release grades to respondents.

5. Collecting Email Addresses:

- If you want to collect email addresses, you can:

- Toggle on "Collect email addresses" in the General tab.

- Choose whether to restrict form access to users within your organization.

6. Response Receipts:

- Enable "Collect email addresses" to send respondents a receipt of their responses.

7. Limiting Responses:

- In the General tab, set response limits:

- "Limit to 1 response" to restrict each respondent to a single submission.

- "Limit to 1 response per user" if collecting email addresses.

8. Respondent Editing:

- In the General tab, toggle on "Edit after submit" to allow respondents to edit their responses after submission.

9. Confirmation Message:

- Customize the confirmation message displayed to respondents after they submit the form.

10. Confirmation Page Options:

- Choose what respondents see after submitting the form:

- "Show a link to submit another response."

- "Publish and show a link to the results of this form."

11. Prefilling a Form:

- If you want to prefill certain fields, use the Prefill tab to generate a prefill link.

12. Language Settings:

- In the Presentation tab, choose the default language for your form.

13. Advanced Settings:

- Access additional settings by clicking on the three dots next to the gear icon. Here, you can:

  - Print a form.

  - Delete a form.

  - View version history.

14. Save Your Settings:

- Ensure to click "Save" after customizing your form settings to apply the changes.

Customizing form settings gives you control over the form's behavior, appearance, and functionality, creating a tailored experience for both creators and respondents.

- **Saving and Accessing Your Form**

aving and accessing your Google Form is crucial for preserving your work and being able to revisit or share it. Here's a guide on how to save and access your form:

Saving Your Form:

1. **Automatic Saving:**

- Google Forms automatically saves your work as you create or edit a form. Edits are saved in real-time, minimizing the risk of losing progress.

2. **Manual Saving:**

- While automatic saving is in place, it's good practice to manually save your form by clicking on the floppy disk icon (Save) in the top-left corner of the Form Editor. This ensures your most recent changes are saved.

3. **Naming Your Form:**

- Click on the title of your form in the top-left corner to give it a descriptive name. This not only helps you identify the form easily but also contributes to organizational clarity in your Google Drive.

Accessing Your Form:

1. **Google Drive:**

• Your Google Forms are stored in Google Drive. To access your form:

• Go to drive.google.com.

• Locate the "Forms" section on the left sidebar.

2. **Recent Documents:**

• On the Google Drive homepage, you'll find a section displaying your recent documents. If you've recently worked on your form, you can access it directly from here.

3. **Search Function:**

• Use the search bar in Google Drive to find your form quickly. Enter keywords related to the form title or content to narrow down the search results.

4. **Shared with Me:**

• If your form was shared with you by someone else, you can find it in the "Shared with Me" section in Google Drive.

5. **Google Forms Homepage:**

•   You can also access your form by going to the Google Forms homepage (forms.google.com) and selecting the desired form from the list of available forms.

6. **Folders:**

•   If you've organized your Google Drive into folders, navigate to the folder where you want to store your form and access it from there.

7. **Recent Items:**

•   On the Google Forms homepage, you'll see a list of recent forms. Click on the desired form to open it.

8. **URL Link:**

•   If you have the URL link to your form, you can access it directly by entering the link in your web browser.

By saving your form regularly and knowing where to access it, you ensure that your work is secure, and you can conveniently continue editing or sharing your form as needed.

CHAPTER 3

DESIGNING ENGAGING FORMS

• Choosing the Right Theme

Choosing the right theme for your Google Form is essential as it sets the tone and visual appeal of your survey or questionnaire. Here's a guide on how to choose the right theme:

1. Accessing Theme Options:

• While in the Form Editor, click on the paint palette icon located in the upper-right corner. This opens the Theme Options menu.

2. Selecting a Theme:

• In the Theme Options menu, you'll see various pre-designed themes. Hover over each theme to see a preview. Click on a theme to apply it to your form.

3. Customizing Colors:

• After selecting a theme, you can further customize its colors. Click on the color palette icon to access the color options. Choose colors that align with your brand or the survey's purpose.

4. Adding Images:

- Some themes allow you to add a custom image to the form header. Click on the image icon to upload or select an image from Google Drive. This is a great way to personalize your form.

5. Previewing Your Theme:

- Before finalizing your theme, click on the eye icon (Preview) to see how it will appear to respondents. This helps you ensure the visual aesthetics match your expectations.

Tips for Choosing the Right Theme:

1. **Consider Your Audience:**

- Think about the preferences and expectations of your audience. A professional theme might be suitable for business-related forms, while a more playful theme could work for surveys targeting a younger audience.

2. **Branding:**

- If the form represents a brand or organization, choose colors and themes that align with the brand's visual identity. Consistent branding enhances recognition and professionalism.

3. **Legibility:**

- Ensure that the chosen theme provides good contrast between text and background colors. Legible forms are more user-friendly and lead to better response rates.

4. **Purpose of the Form:**

• The theme should complement the purpose of your form. For example, a serious topic may warrant a more subdued theme, while a fun and engaging theme could be suitable for a casual survey.

5. **Accessibility:**

• Consider accessibility by choosing themes with clear, easy-to-read fonts and color combinations. This ensures that your form is inclusive and can be easily understood by a diverse audience.

6. **Consistency:**

• If you're creating multiple forms, consider maintaining a consistent theme across them. This creates a cohesive look and reinforces your brand or identity.

7. **Adaptability:**

• Choose a theme that looks good on various devices. Google Forms are often accessed from different screen sizes, so a responsive theme ensures a positive user experience.

By carefully selecting the right theme, you enhance the visual appeal of your Google Form, making it more engaging and aligned with your goals.

- **Adding Images and Videos**

Enhance the visual appeal and clarity of your Google Form by adding images and videos. Here's a guide on how to incorporate multimedia elements into your form:

Adding Images:

1. **Access the Form Editor:**

- Open your Google Form and navigate to the Form Editor.

2. **Click on the Image Icon:**

- While editing a question or form header, click on the image icon. This opens the "Image" menu.

3. **Upload or Select an Image:**

- Choose whether to upload an image from your device or select an image from your Google Drive. Follow the prompts to add the image to your form.

4. **Adjust Image Size:**

- After adding the image, you can click on it to adjust its size. Drag the corners to resize the image according to your preferences.

5. **Image Positioning:**

• Use the alignment options to position the image to the left, center, or right of the form or question.

6. **Alt Text:**

• Consider adding descriptive alt text to your images. This is useful for accessibility purposes, allowing users with screen readers to understand the content of the image.

Adding Videos:

1. **Access the Form Editor:**

• Open your Google Form and navigate to the Form Editor.

2. **Click on the Video Icon:**

• While editing a question or form header, click on the video icon. This opens the "Insert video" menu.

3. **Paste Video URL:**

• Copy and paste the URL of the video you want to embed. This can be a YouTube video or a video hosted on Google Drive.

4. **Adjust Video Size:**

• After adding the video, you can click on it to adjust its size. Drag the corners to resize the video based on your preferences.

5. **Video Positioning:**

• Use the alignment options to position the video to the left, center, or right of the form or question.

6. **Preview Your Form:**

• Before finalizing, click on the eye icon (Preview) to see how the images and videos will appear to respondents. Ensure they enhance the overall user experience.

Tips for Adding Images and Videos:

1. **Relevance:**

• Ensure that images and videos are relevant to the content of the form. They should provide additional context or clarification to respondents.

2. **File Size:**

• Optimize image and video file sizes to maintain a smooth user experience. Large files may slow down the loading time of your form.

3.   **Consistency:**

•   Maintain a consistent visual style. Choose images and videos that align with the overall theme and branding of your form.

4.   **Accessibility:**

•   Consider accessibility by providing alternative text for images and ensuring that videos have captions or transcripts.

5.   **Test on Different Devices:**

•   Preview your form on different devices to ensure that images and videos are displayed correctly and do not compromise the form's responsiveness.

By incorporating images and videos strategically, you can create a more engaging and informative Google Form, providing a richer experience for your respondents.

•   **Formatting and Styling Options**

Formatting and styling your Google Form can enhance its visual appeal and improve the overall user experience. Here's a guide on how to use formatting and styling options:

Text Formatting:

1. Bold, Italicize, and Underline:

- Highlight the text you want to format, then use the formatting toolbar to bold (B), italicize (I), or underline (U) the selected text.

2. Font Size:

- Use the dropdown menu in the formatting toolbar to change the font size of selected text.

3. Font Color:

- Change the color of your text by using the "A" icon in the formatting toolbar. Select the desired color to apply it to the selected text.

Paragraph Formatting:

1. Text Alignment:

- Align text to the left, center, or right using the alignment icons in the formatting toolbar.

2. Bulleted and Numbered Lists:

- Create bulleted or numbered lists by selecting the corresponding icons in the formatting toolbar.

3. **Line Spacing:**

•   Adjust line spacing by selecting the line spacing icon in the formatting toolbar.

Form Styling:

1. **Theme Options:**

•   Click on the paint palette icon to access Theme Options. Choose a theme that suits the purpose and aesthetics of your form.

2. **Background Color:**

•   Change the background color of your form by clicking on the paint palette icon, then selecting the color palette icon. Choose a background color that complements your theme.

3. **Header Image:**

•   Add a header image to your form for a personalized touch. Click on the image icon in the Form Editor to upload or select an image.

Section and Page Styling:

1. **Section Background Color:**

•   Click on the color palette icon next to a section title to change the background color of that section.

2. **Page Background Color:**

•   Similar to section styling, you can click on the color palette icon next to a page title to change the background color of that page.

Previewing Your Form:

1. **Preview Mode:**

•   Click on the eye icon (Preview) to see how your formatted and styled form will appear to respondents. This helps you ensure that the styling choices enhance the user experience.

Tips for Formatting and Styling:

1. **Consistency:**

•   Maintain a consistent style throughout your form. Use similar fonts, colors, and formatting options to create a cohesive and professional look.

2. **Readability:**

•   Prioritize readability by choosing legible fonts, appropriate font sizes, and contrasting colors for text and background.

3. **Brand Alignment:**

•   If the form represents a brand or organization, align the formatting and styling with the brand's visual identity.

4.   **Accessibility:**

- Consider accessibility by ensuring that your chosen colors and fonts are accessible to all users, including those with visual impairments.

By leveraging formatting and styling options, you can create a visually appealing and user-friendly Google Form that effectively communicates your message to respondents.

- **Making Your Form User-Friendly**

Creating a user-friendly Google Form ensures a positive experience for respondents and increases the likelihood of receiving accurate and valuable responses. Here's a guide on how to make your form user-friendly:

1. Clear and Concise Form Title:

- Provide a descriptive and clear title for your form. It should give respondents a quick understanding of the form's purpose.

2. Organized Structure:

- Use sections and page breaks to organize your form logically. A well-structured form is easier to navigate and encourages completion.

3. Simple and Direct Language:

- Use straightforward and easy-to-understand language in your questions. Avoid jargon or complex terminology that may confuse respondents.

4. Progressive Disclosure:

- Present questions in a logical order, following a natural flow. Start with simple and less personal questions before moving on to more complex or sensitive ones.

5. Use of Headers and Descriptions:

- Add headers and descriptions to provide context and instructions for each section or set of questions. Clear instructions reduce confusion.

6. Responsive Design:

- Ensure that your form is mobile-friendly. Google Forms automatically adapts to different devices, but preview your form on various screens to confirm responsiveness.

7. Limit Question Types:

- Use a variety of question types, but avoid overwhelming respondents with too many complex options. Stick to the most relevant question types for your survey.

8. Required vs. Optional Questions:

- Clearly indicate which questions are required and which are optional. This transparency helps respondents understand the level of commitment required.

9. Progress Indicators:

- If your form is lengthy, use progress indicators to show respondents how far they are in the completion process. This prevents them from feeling overwhelmed.

10. Smart Use of Images and Videos:

- Integrate images and videos judiciously. Use visuals to enhance understanding, provide examples, or make the form more engaging.

11. Preview Option:

- Encourage users to preview their responses before submission. This allows them to review their answers and make any necessary changes.

12. Thank You Message:

- Customize the thank-you message that respondents see after submitting the form. Express appreciation and provide any additional information or next steps.

13. Testing the Form:

• Before sharing the form, test it thoroughly to ensure that all elements are functioning as expected. This includes checking question logic, required fields, and the overall user experience.

14. Accessibility Considerations:

• Ensure that your form is accessible to users with disabilities. This includes using clear and descriptive labels, providing alternative text for images, and choosing accessible color contrasts.

15. Share Options:

• Opt for easy sharing options. Generate a shareable link, embed the form on a website, or send direct email invitations based on the most convenient method for your audience.

By implementing these user-friendly practices, you create a positive interaction with your Google Form, leading to higher response rates and more valuable data.

• Previewing and Testing Your Form

Before sharing your Google Form with respondents, it's crucial to preview and test it to ensure a smooth and error-free experience. Here's a step-by-step guide on how to preview and test your form:

1. Access the Form Editor:

- Open your Google Form and navigate to the Form Editor.

2. Previewing Your Form:

- Click on the eye icon (Preview) in the top-right corner of the Form Editor. This opens a preview of your form, allowing you to see how it will appear to respondents.

3. Test Each Question Type:

- Go through each question type in your form to make sure they function as intended. Test multiple-choice questions, text questions, and any other question types you've included.

4. Check Logic and Branching:

- If you've implemented logic or branching in your form (showing or hiding questions based on responses), test this functionality to ensure it works seamlessly.

5. Verify Required Questions:

- Confirm that required questions are appropriately marked, and the form prevents submission if respondents skip them.

6. Test Validation Rules:

- If you've set up validation rules for specific questions, test these to ensure they accurately validate responses according to your criteria.

7. Check Section and Page Breaks:

- If you've used section breaks or page breaks to organize your form, verify that they create a logical and user-friendly flow.

8. Preview on Different Devices:

- Preview your form on different devices, such as desktops, laptops, tablets, and smartphones, to ensure a responsive design and optimal user experience.

9. Test Image and Video Integration:

- If you've added images or videos to your form, verify that they load correctly and enhance the overall presentation.

10. Test Submission Process: - Complete your form as a respondent would, including submitting responses. Confirm that the submission process works smoothly and that respondents see the appropriate thank-you message.

11. Review Thank-You Message:

- Customize and review the thank-you message that respondents see after submitting the form. Ensure it provides relevant information or next steps.

12. Check Form Settings:

- Review the form settings, including access permissions, response collection, and any advanced settings you've configured.

13. Share Test Link:

- Before sharing the form with your intended audience, consider creating a test link and sharing it with a small group of colleagues or friends for additional feedback.

14. Analyze Results:

- If your form is set up to collect responses in a linked Google Sheets spreadsheet, review the spreadsheet to ensure that responses are recorded accurately.

15. Iterate Based on Feedback:

- If you receive feedback from your preview and testing, be open to making necessary adjustments. Iterate on your form to enhance its usability and effectiveness.

By thoroughly previewing and testing your Google Form, you can identify and address any issues before sharing it with your target audience, ensuring a positive and error-free user experience.

CHAPTER 4

ADVANCED FORM FEATURES

- **Logic and Branching**

Logic and branching in Google Forms allow you to create a more personalized and dynamic survey experience. By showing or hiding questions based on respondents' answers, you can tailor the form to their specific needs. Here's a guide on how to implement logic and branching in your form:

1. Access the Form Editor:

- Open your Google Form and navigate to the Form Editor.

2. Create or Edit a Question:

- Click on the question you want to apply logic to or add a new question to your form.

3. Click on the Three Dots:

- Next to the question, click on the three dots to access additional options.

4. Select "Go to section based on answer":

- Choose "Go to section based on answer" from the dropdown menu.

5. Create Sections:

- If you haven't created sections yet, you'll be prompted to create sections. Sections are used to organize questions and set the conditions for branching.

6. Name the Sections:

- Give each section a descriptive name that reflects the criteria for branching. For example, you might have sections named "High Interest," "Low Interest," or "Additional Details."

7. Set Conditions:

- For each answer option in the question, select the section to which respondents should be directed. This establishes the conditions for branching.

8. Add Questions to Sections:

- In each section, add the relevant questions that should be shown based on the conditions you've set. Questions in different sections won't be visible simultaneously.

9. Test Logic and Branching:

- Click on the eye icon (Preview) to test how your logic and branching work. Respond as a respondent would and verify that the form directs you to the appropriate sections based on your answers.

Tips for Using Logic and Branching:

1. **Plan Your Survey Flow:**

•   Before implementing logic and branching, plan the flow of your survey. Consider the logical sequence of questions and how branching can personalize the experience.

2. **Use Conditional Logic Wisely:**

•   Be strategic in applying conditional logic. Use it for questions where respondents' answers genuinely determine the relevance of subsequent questions.

3. **Test Thoroughly:**

•   Test your form extensively to ensure that logic and branching work as intended. Verify that questions are hidden or shown based on the conditions you've set.

4. **Consider Default Sections:**

•   Set default sections for respondents who don't meet any of the conditions. This ensures they are directed to an appropriate section even if their answers don't match specific conditions.

5. **Clear Instructions:**

- Provide clear instructions to respondents about how the survey works, especially if certain questions will be hidden or shown based on their answers.

6. Iterate Based on Feedback:

- If you receive feedback from previewing or testing, be open to making adjustments. Iterate on your logic and branching to enhance the survey experience.

By incorporating logic and branching into your Google Form, you create a more tailored and engaging survey for respondents, increasing the relevance and accuracy of the data you collect.

- **Sections and Page Breaks**

Sections and page breaks in Google Forms help organize your survey, making it more user-friendly and logical. Here's a guide on how to use sections and page breaks effectively:

1. Access the Form Editor:

- Open your Google Form and navigate to the Form Editor.

2. Inserting a Section Break:

- Click on the place in your form where you want to add a section break. Click on the "+" icon on the right side of the Form Editor, and then select "Section."

3. Naming Sections:

- After adding a section break, you'll be prompted to give the section a name. Provide a descriptive name that reflects the content or purpose of the section.

4. Adding Questions to Sections:

- Add questions to the section by clicking on the section title, then clicking on the "+" icon to add questions or dragging existing questions into the section.

5. Adjusting Section Order:

- Drag and drop sections to rearrange the order. This helps in creating a logical flow for respondents.

6. Adding a Page Break:

- If you want to separate a section onto a new page, click on the question where you want the new page to begin. Click on the three dots in the question options and select "Page break."

7. Previewing Sections:

- Click on the eye icon (Preview) to see how the sections and page breaks will appear to respondents. This allows you to verify the survey's flow and organization.

Tips for Using Sections and Page Breaks:

1. **Logical Organization:**

- Use sections to logically organize your form. For example, you might have sections for personal information, preferences, and feedback.

2. **Clear Section Names:**

- Provide clear and descriptive names for each section to guide respondents and enhance the overall user experience.

3. **Avoid Lengthy Sections:**

- If possible, avoid creating overly long sections. Breaking them into smaller sections with a clear focus improves readability and engagement.

4. **Use Page Breaks Sparingly:**

- While page breaks can be helpful, use them sparingly. Only introduce a new page when transitioning to a significantly different section or topic.

5. **Review Flow:**

- Preview your form to review the flow between sections. Ensure that respondents can navigate through the survey seamlessly.

6. **Consider Theme Changes:**

- If different sections of your survey have distinct themes or topics, consider changing the theme or colors to visually signal the transition.

7. Test on Different Devices:

- Test your form on various devices to ensure that sections and page breaks are displayed correctly and do not disrupt the overall user experience.

8. Iterate Based on Feedback:

- If you receive feedback from testing or previewing, be open to making adjustments to section organization or page breaks. Iteration improves the overall survey design.

By using sections and page breaks strategically, you can create a well-organized and user-friendly Google Form that enhances the respondent experience and facilitates efficient data collection.

- **Required Questions and Validation**

Requiring certain questions and using validation in your Google Form ensures that respondents provide accurate and complete information. Here's a guide on how to set up required questions and validation:

1. Access the Form Editor:

- Open your Google Form and navigate to the Form Editor.

2. Making a Question Required:

- Click on the question you want to make required. In the question options, toggle on the "Required" switch. This ensures respondents cannot submit the form without answering the question.

3. Setting Validation Rules:

- To set up validation for a question:

  - Click on the question.

  - Click on the three dots to access additional options.

  - Select "Validation."

4. Choose Validation Criteria:

- In the validation settings, choose the type of validation you want:

  - **Text:** Specify if the response should be a number, text, date, or length of text.

    - **Number:** Set a range for numeric responses.

    - **Date:** Specify a date range.

    - **Regular expression:** Use advanced patterns for validation.

5. Define Validation Criteria:

- Depending on the validation type selected, define the criteria. For example, if setting a text validation for an email address, you can specify that the response must match the pattern of an email address.

6. Customize Error Messages:

- Customize the error message that respondents see if they enter an invalid response. Make the error message clear and instructive.

7. Test Validation:

- Before sharing your form, test the validation rules to ensure they work as intended. Try entering both valid and invalid responses to verify the error messages.

Tips for Using Required Questions and Validation:

1. **Strategic Use of Required Questions:**

- Make questions required strategically. If a question is essential for your data collection, mark it as required. However, avoid making every question mandatory to prevent survey fatigue.

2. **Clear Instructions:**

- Provide clear instructions for required questions. Let respondents know why certain questions are mandatory and how their answers will be used.

3. Use Validation for Data Accuracy:

- Implement validation rules for questions where data accuracy is crucial. For example, use number validation for age or date validation for event dates.

4. Consider Default Answers:

- For multiple-choice questions, consider setting a default answer if none of the provided options apply. This ensures that respondents actively choose a relevant response.

5. Test Thoroughly:

- Test your form thoroughly to ensure that required questions and validation work as intended. Consider scenarios where respondents might try to bypass requirements.

6. Balance User Experience:

- While data accuracy is essential, balance it with a positive user experience. Avoid overly restrictive validation rules that may frustrate respondents.

7. Iterate Based on Feedback:

- If you receive feedback during testing, be open to adjusting required questions and validation rules. Iterative improvements contribute to a more effective form.

By incorporating required questions and validation, you ensure the completeness and accuracy of the data collected through your Google Form, ultimately enhancing the reliability of your survey results.

- **Adding Collaborators to Your Form**

Collaboration can streamline the form creation process and improve the overall quality of your Google Form. Here's a guide on how to add collaborators to your form:

1. Access the Form Editor:

- Open your Google Form and navigate to the Form Editor.

2. Click on the "Collaborate" Button:

- In the top-right corner of the Form Editor, click on the "Collaborate" button. It looks like a person icon with a "+" sign.

3. Enter Collaborators' Email Addresses:

- In the "Share with others" dialog box, enter the email addresses of the individuals you want to collaborate with. You can add multiple collaborators.

4. Choose Permission Levels:

- Next to each email address, select the permission level for each collaborator. There are three permission levels:

- **Editor:** Can edit the form, including adding or deleting questions.

- **Commenter:** Can view the form and add comments but cannot make direct edits.

- **Viewer:** Can only view the form without editing or commenting.

5. Add a Message (Optional):

- You can include a message to your collaborators to provide context or specific instructions.

6. Click "Send":

- Once you've added collaborators and set permission levels, click on the "Send" button. Collaborators will receive an email invitation.

7. Collaborators' Access:

- Collaborators can access the form by clicking on the link in the email invitation or by opening the shared form from their Google Drive.

Tips for Collaborating on Google Forms:

1. **Effective Communication:**

- Communicate with your collaborators about the purpose of the form, the target audience, and any specific requirements. Clear communication ensures everyone is on the same page.

2. **Version History:**

- Monitor changes using the version history feature. It allows you to review edits made by collaborators and revert to previous versions if needed.

3. **Commenting Feature:**

- Encourage collaborators to use the commenting feature to provide feedback or ask questions. This helps in maintaining a transparent collaboration process.

4. **Shared Folder:**

• Consider creating a shared folder in Google Drive for the form and related documents. This centralizes resources and makes collaboration more organized.

5. Assign Responsibilities:

• If multiple collaborators are working on different sections of the form, assign responsibilities to avoid overlap and ensure efficiency.

6. Regular Check-Ins:

• Schedule regular check-ins or meetings to discuss progress, address any challenges, and make collaborative decisions.

7. Respecting Permissions:

• Be mindful of the permission levels assigned to collaborators. Ensure that individuals with editing capabilities are trusted contributors.

8. Backup Your Form:

• Before major edits or changes, consider making a backup copy of your form. This ensures that you have a snapshot of the form at various stages of development.

By leveraging the collaboration features in Google Forms, you can benefit from the collective expertise and contributions of your collaborators, resulting in a more polished and effective form.

- **Using Templates for Efficiency**

Google Forms offers a variety of templates that can save you time and provide a starting point for creating different types of forms. Here's a guide on how to use templates for efficiency:

1. Access Google Forms:

- Open Google Forms in your web browser and click on the "+" (plus) sign to create a new form.

2. Choose a Template:

- Instead of starting with a blank form, click on the "Template gallery" option. This opens a gallery of pre-designed templates.

3. Browse or Search:

- Browse through the available templates or use the search bar to find a template that suits your needs. Templates cover a range of purposes, from event planning to feedback forms.

4. Preview the Template:

- Click on a template to preview its contents. This allows you to see the structure and questions included in the template.

5. Use Template:

- If the template fits your requirements, click on the "Use template" button. This creates a copy of the template in your Google Drive.

6. Customize the Form:

- Once the template is added to your Google Drive, customize it to meet your specific needs. Edit questions, add or remove sections, and personalize the form according to your requirements.

7. Preview and Test:

- Before sharing the form, preview and test it to ensure that the customized template functions as intended. Verify question logic, required fields, and overall user experience.

Tips for Using Templates:

1. Explore Different Categories:

- Google Forms templates cover various categories, including education, business, and personal use. Explore different categories to find a template that aligns with your goals.

2. Adapt to Your Needs:

- Templates are customizable. Don't hesitate to modify the template to better suit your specific requirements. Add or remove questions, change themes, and adjust settings as needed.

3. **Combine Templates:**

- If no single template perfectly fits your needs, consider combining elements from multiple templates. This allows you to create a form that's tailored to your unique requirements.

4. **Create Your Own Template:**

- If you frequently use a specific format or set of questions, consider creating your own template. Save it in Google Drive and reuse it for future forms.

5. **Check for Updates:**

- Periodically check for updates to Google Forms templates. Google may add new templates or improve existing ones, providing you with more options and features.

6. **Collaborate on Templates:**

- If you're working on a form with collaborators, consider creating a template together. This ensures that everyone starts with a standardized structure.

7. **Share Your Templates:**

- If you create a customized template that you find particularly useful, share it with others in your organization. This promotes consistency and efficiency across projects.

By leveraging Google Forms templates, you can jumpstart your form creation process, saving time and ensuring a well-designed and functional form for your specific needs.

CHAPTER 5

COLLECTING RESPONSES

- **Sharing Your Form**

Once your Google Form is ready, it's time to share it with your intended audience. Here's a guide on how to effectively share your form:

1. Access the Form Editor:

- Open your Google Form and navigate to the Form Editor.

2. Click on the "Send" Button:

- In the top-right corner of the Form Editor, click on the "Send" button.

3. Choose a Sharing Option:

- Google Forms provides various sharing options. Choose the method that best suits your needs:

- **Link Sharing:**

- Click on the link icon to generate a shareable link. You can copy and paste this link to share with your audience. Choose the level of access (Anyone with the link can respond, or Restrict to your organization).

- **Email:**

- Click on the email icon to send invitations directly via email. Enter the email addresses of your respondents, include a message, and send the invitations.

- **Embed HTML:**

- If you have a website or blog, you can click on the embed icon to get an HTML code. This allows you to embed the form directly on your website.

- **Social Media:**

- Use the social media icons to share your form on various platforms. Click on the desired platform, and follow the prompts to share the form.

- **QR Code:**

- Generate a QR code for your form by clicking on the QR code icon. This is useful for offline promotion or easy access via mobile devices.

4. Set Form Permissions:

- If you're sharing the form within your organization, consider adjusting the permissions under "Settings." Choose who can respond to the form (Anyone in the organization, Anyone with the link, or Only people in your organization).

5. Collect Responses in a Spreadsheet:

• If you want to collect responses in a linked Google Sheets spreadsheet, click on the Google Sheets icon. This creates a connected spreadsheet where responses will be automatically recorded.

Tips for Sharing Your Form:

1. **Customize the Message:**

• When sending email invitations or sharing on social media, customize the message. Provide context, explain the purpose of the form, and encourage participation.

2. **Share Responsibly:**

• Be mindful of privacy and permissions. Only share forms with the appropriate level of access, especially when dealing with sensitive information.

3. **Promote on Multiple Channels:**

• To maximize responses, promote your form across multiple channels. Share it via email, social media, and any relevant online platforms.

4. **Include a Call to Action:**

• Clearly communicate what you want respondents to do. Include a call to action in your message, whether it's to complete a survey, submit feedback, or provide information.

5. **Monitor Responses:**

- Regularly check the responses in your linked Google Sheets spreadsheet. This allows you to analyze data in real-time and make informed decisions.

6. **Encourage Sharing:**

- If appropriate, encourage respondents to share the form with others. This can help increase the reach and diversity of responses.

7. **Test the Form Link:**

- Before sharing widely, test the form link to ensure that it opens correctly and that respondents can access it without issues.

8. **Set a Deadline:**

- If your form has a deadline for responses, clearly communicate this in your sharing messages. This adds a sense of urgency and encourages timely participation.

By using the various sharing options and following these tips, you can effectively distribute your Google Form and gather the responses you need.

- **Emailing Form Invitations**

Sending email invitations for your Google Form is a personalized and targeted way to reach your audience. Here's a step-by-step guide on how to email form invitations:

1. Access the Form Editor:

- Open your Google Form and navigate to the Form Editor.

2. Click on the "Send" Button:

- In the top-right corner of the Form Editor, click on the "Send" button.

3. Choose the Email Icon:

- Click on the email icon to send invitations via email.

4. Enter Email Addresses:

- In the "To" field, enter the email addresses of the individuals you want to invite. You can enter multiple email addresses, separating them with commas.

5. Customize the Subject:

- Customize the email subject to grab recipients' attention. Make it clear and relevant to the purpose of your form.

6. Compose Your Message:

• Craft a personalized message in the email body. Explain the purpose of the form, provide any necessary context, and include a call to action encouraging recipients to respond.

7. Insert Form Link:

• Insert the form link within your email message. You can do this by copying the link from the Form Editor and pasting it into the email body.

8. Send Invitations:

• Once you've customized the email, click on the "Send" button to dispatch the invitations. Recipients will receive an email with your message and a link to the form.

Tips for Emailing Form Invitations:

1. Personalize Your Message:

• Tailor your email message to your audience. Personalization adds a human touch and increases the likelihood of engagement.

2. Explain the Importance:

• Clearly explain why the recipient's input is valuable. Whether it's for a survey, feedback, or information gathering, conveying the importance of their response can motivate participation.

3. **Include a Deadline:**

- If applicable, include a deadline for responding to the form. This adds a sense of urgency and encourages timely completion.

4. **Test the Email:**

- Before sending to your entire list, send a test email to yourself or a colleague. This allows you to check the formatting and ensure that the form link works correctly.

5. **Follow Up:**

- If you don't receive responses within a reasonable timeframe, consider sending a follow-up email as a gentle reminder. Include a thank-you message for those who have already responded.

6. **Use Bcc for Privacy:**

- If you're sending invitations to a group, consider using the Bcc (blind carbon copy) field to protect the privacy of recipients' email addresses.

7. **Track Responses:**

- Monitor the responses in your Google Form linked spreadsheet. This allows you to track who has responded and analyze the data as it comes in.

8. **Provide Support Contact:**

•   Include contact information in case recipients have questions or need assistance. This can increase trust and willingness to participate.

By following these steps and tips, you can effectively email invitations for your Google Form, maximizing the chances of receiving meaningful responses from your audience.

•   **Embedding Forms on Websites**

Embedding your Google Form directly on your website allows respondents to fill out the form without leaving the webpage. Here's a guide on how to embed forms on websites:

1. Access the Form Editor:

•   Open your Google Form and navigate to the Form Editor.

2. Click on the Embed Icon:

•   In the top-right corner of the Form Editor, click on the embed icon (</>). This opens the embed options.

3. Copy the Embed Code:

•   Copy the HTML code provided in the embed options. This code is what you'll use to embed the form on your website.

4. Access Your Website's HTML:

- Go to the backend of your website where you can edit the HTML code. This might be through a content management system (CMS) like WordPress, or directly in the HTML file if you're using a static website.

5. Paste the Embed Code:

- In your website's HTML, find the location where you want to embed the form. Paste the copied embed code at that location.

6. Save or Update Your Website:

- Save or update the changes on your website. This might involve clicking a "Save" button in your CMS or updating the HTML file directly.

7. Preview the Embedded Form:

- Open your website in a browser and navigate to the page where you embedded the form. Check to ensure that the form displays correctly.

Tips for Embedding Forms on Websites:

1. **Responsive Design:**

- Ensure that your website and the embedded form are responsive to different screen sizes. Google Forms is designed to be mobile-friendly, but it's essential to check how it appears on various devices.

2. **Embed on Relevant Pages:**

• Embed the form on pages of your website that are most relevant to the form's purpose. For example, if it's a feedback form, consider embedding it on your "Contact Us" or "Feedback" page.

3. **Test the Embedded Form:**

• Before making it live, test the embedded form to ensure that respondents can fill it out seamlessly. Check for any issues with form submission or display.

4. **Customize Embed Options:**

• In the Form Editor, you can customize certain embed options, such as whether to show a progress bar or submit another response. Adjust these options based on your preferences.

5. **Security Considerations:**

• Be mindful of the security implications of embedding forms, especially if you're collecting sensitive information. Ensure that your website has proper security measures in place.

6. **Update Form Changes:**

• If you make changes to your Google Form (e.g., adding or modifying questions), you may need to update the embedded code on your website to reflect these changes.

7. **Consider Accessibility:**

• Ensure that the embedded form is accessible to users with disabilities. Google Forms itself is designed with accessibility in mind, but it's essential to confirm this in the context of your website.

By embedding your Google Form on your website, you create a seamless and integrated experience for respondents, encouraging participation and making it convenient for them to provide feedback or information.

• **Generating QR Codes for Mobile Access**

Creating a QR code for your Google Form provides a quick and convenient way for respondents to access the form using their mobile devices. Here's a guide on how to generate QR codes for mobile access:

1. Access the Form Editor:

• Open your Google Form and navigate to the Form Editor.

2. Click on the QR Code Icon:

• In the top-right corner of the Form Editor, click on the QR code icon. This opens the QR code options.

3. Customize QR Code Settings (Optional):

• You can customize the QR code settings, such as the color and size. Adjust these settings based on your preferences.

4. Download the QR Code:

• Click on the "Download" button to download the QR code as an image file (usually in PNG format).

5. Save the QR Code Image:

• Save the downloaded image to your computer. This image is the QR code that, when scanned, will direct users to your Google Form.

6. Use the QR Code:

• Incorporate the QR code into your materials, such as print materials, presentations, or digital communications. Users can scan the QR code with their mobile devices to access the form directly.

Tips for Generating QR Codes:

1. **Test the QR Code:**

• Before sharing the QR code widely, test it to ensure that it correctly directs users to your Google Form. Confirm that the form is accessible and functional.

2. **Include Instructions:**

• If the audience may not be familiar with scanning QR codes, include brief instructions on how to do so. Mention that they can use their device's camera or a QR code scanner app.

3. **Choose a Visible Location:**

• When using the QR code in print materials, presentations, or online content, place it in a visible location. Ensure that users can easily scan it with their mobile devices.

4. **Consider QR Code Size:**

• Depending on where you plan to use the QR code, consider the appropriate size. In print materials, a larger QR code may be necessary for optimal scanning.

5. **Link to a Mobile-Friendly Form:**

• Ensure that the Google Form you're linking to is mobile-friendly. Google Forms are designed to be responsive, but it's always a good idea to test the mobile experience.

6. **Update QR Code for Changes:**

• If you make changes to your Google Form, such as adding or modifying questions, generate a new QR code to reflect these changes.

7. **Share Digitally and Physically:**

• Use the QR code in both digital and physical contexts. For example, include it in an email newsletter and print materials for comprehensive reach.

8. **Track QR Code Usage:**

- If you're interested in tracking the usage of the QR code, consider using a QR code tracking service. This provides insights into how many times the code has been scanned.

By incorporating QR codes, you offer a convenient way for users to access your Google Form using their mobile devices, enhancing accessibility and participation.

- **Monitoring Response Metrics in Real-time**

Monitoring response metrics in real-time allows you to gain insights into how your Google Form is performing and make informed decisions based on the data collected. Here's a guide on how to monitor response metrics in real-time:

1. Access the Google Form:

- Open your Google Form and navigate to the Form Editor.

2. Click on the "Responses" Tab:

- In the Form Editor, click on the "Responses" tab at the top.

3. View Summary of Responses:

- The "Responses" tab provides a summary of responses, including the total number of responses and a graphical representation of response trends over time.

4. Access the Spreadsheet:

- If you linked your form to a Google Sheets spreadsheet, you can click on the "View responses in Sheets" option to open the linked spreadsheet. This allows for more detailed analysis and manipulation of the response data.

5. Set Up Notifications (Optional):

- If you want to receive email notifications when someone submits a response, click on the "More options" (three dots) and select "Get email notifications for new responses."

6. Use Google Sheets Features:

- In the linked Google Sheets spreadsheet, take advantage of the features for data analysis, such as sorting, filtering, and creating charts. These tools can help you understand response patterns and trends.

7. Monitor Individual Questions:

- In the "Questions" tab within the "Responses" section, you can view individual question metrics. This includes the distribution of responses for each question.

8. Explore Google Forms Add-ons:

- Consider exploring Google Forms add-ons that provide additional analytics and reporting features. Some add-ons offer advanced analytics and visualization options for a more comprehensive view of response metrics.

Tips for Monitoring Response Metrics:

1. **Regularly Check Responses:**

• Make it a habit to regularly check the responses to your form. This allows you to stay informed about the progress of your survey or data collection.

2. **Set Benchmarks:**

• Establish benchmarks for response rates and completion times based on your goals. This helps you assess the performance of your form and identify areas for improvement.

3. **Use Data Filters:**

• In Google Sheets, use data filters to focus on specific subsets of responses. This is helpful when analyzing responses based on certain criteria or demographics.

4. **Export and Share Reports:**

• Export summary reports or charts from Google Sheets and share them with stakeholders or team members. This provides a visual representation of response metrics.

5. **Identify Drop-off Points:**

• Look for patterns in the data that indicate drop-off points or areas where respondents may disengage. This information can guide improvements to your form.

6. **Leverage Time-Based Analysis:**

• Analyze responses over time to identify peak submission periods or trends. This can be useful for planning future surveys or optimizing promotional efforts.

7. **Iterate Based on Insights:**

• Based on the insights gathered from response metrics, iterate on your form if needed. Make adjustments to improve the user experience and gather more meaningful data.

By actively monitoring response metrics in real-time and utilizing the tools available in Google Forms and Google Sheets, you can make data-driven decisions and continuously optimize your form for better results.

CHAPTER 6

ANALYZING AND EXPORTING RESPONSES

- **Overview of Response Summary**

The Response Summary in Google Forms provides a quick snapshot of key metrics and trends related to the responses received for your form. Here's an overview of the Response Summary:

1. Accessing the Response Summary:

- To access the Response Summary, open your Google Form and navigate to the Form Editor. Click on the "Responses" tab at the top.

2. Total Responses:

- The Response Summary prominently displays the total number of responses received for your form. This gives you an immediate sense of the overall engagement.

3. Response Trends:

- Graphical representations, such as line charts or bar graphs, visualize the trends in response submissions over time. This helps you identify any patterns or fluctuations in the response rate.

4. Time-Based Metrics:

• If your form collects responses over a specific period, the Response Summary may display metrics related to submission times. This includes the distribution of responses across different days or hours.

5. Average Completion Time:

• The average completion time provides insights into how long respondents typically spend completing the form. This metric can be valuable for assessing user engagement.

6. Individual Question Metrics:

• Within the Response Summary, you can explore metrics for individual questions. This includes the distribution of responses for each question, helping you understand the variation in answers.

7. Downloadable Data:

• If your form is linked to a Google Sheets spreadsheet, you can download the response data for more in-depth analysis. This allows you to manipulate the data, create custom reports, and perform advanced calculations.

8. Additional Options:

• Depending on the specific features available in the current version of Google Forms, the Response Summary may offer additional options or insights. For example, you may have access to features like email notifications for new responses or integration with other Google Workspace tools.

Tips for Using the Response Summary:

1. **Regularly Review Responses:**

•   Make it a habit to regularly review the Response Summary to stay informed about the progress of your form. This is particularly important during active data collection periods.

2. **Identify Patterns and Trends:**

•   Use the graphical representations to identify patterns and trends in response submissions. Understanding when responses peak or decline can inform your survey strategy.

3. **Compare Across Questions:**

•   Compare the distribution of responses across individual questions. This helps you identify which questions resonate most with respondents and which may need clarification or improvement.

4. **Utilize Time-Based Metrics:**

•   If your form is time-sensitive, leverage time-based metrics to analyze response patterns over different periods. This can be valuable for planning future surveys or events.

5. **Download Data for Deeper Analysis:**

•   If you need more granular insights, download the response data and use Google Sheets or other analysis tools to perform deeper analysis and visualization.

6. **Iterate Based on Insights:**

•   Use the insights gathered from the Response Summary to iterate on your form if needed. Consider making adjustments to improve the user experience and gather more meaningful data.

By utilizing the features available in the Response Summary, you can efficiently monitor and analyze response metrics, allowing you to make informed decisions and optimize your Google Form for better results.

•   **Filtering and Sorting Responses**

Filtering and sorting responses in Google Forms allow you to organize and analyze the collected data more effectively. Here's a guide on how to filter and sort responses:

Filtering Responses:

1. **Access the Google Sheets Spreadsheet:**

- If your form is linked to a Google Sheets spreadsheet, click on the "View responses in Sheets" option in the "Responses" tab of the Form Editor.

2. **Use the Data Menu:**

- In Google Sheets, go to the "Data" menu in the toolbar.

3. **Select "Create a Filter":**

- Click on "Create a filter." This adds filter options to each column header in the spreadsheet.

4. **Filter by Criteria:**

- Click on the filter icon in the column header of the data you want to filter. You can then select specific criteria to filter the responses. For example, you can filter responses based on a range of dates, specific answer choices, or numerical values.

5. **Apply Multiple Filters:**

- You can apply filters to multiple columns simultaneously. This is useful for creating more complex criteria and refining your data analysis.

6. **Clear Filters:**

- To remove filters, click on the filter icon again and select "Clear filter."

Sorting Responses:

1. **Access the Google Sheets Spreadsheet:**

• If your form is linked to a Google Sheets spreadsheet, click on the "View responses in Sheets" option in the "Responses" tab of the Form Editor.

2. **Use the Data Menu:**

• In Google Sheets, go to the "Data" menu in the toolbar.

3. **Select "Sort Range":**

• Click on "Sort range" to open the sorting options.

4. **Choose Sorting Criteria:**

• Specify the column you want to use as the sorting criteria. You can choose to sort in ascending or descending order.

5. **Apply Additional Sorting:**

• You can apply additional sorting criteria by clicking on "Add another sort column." This is useful for sorting responses based on multiple factors.

6. **Undo Sorting:**

• If you need to undo the sorting, click on the "Undo" button in the toolbar.

Tips for Filtering and Sorting Responses:

1. **Focus on Relevant Data:**

• Filter responses to focus on specific subsets of data that are most relevant to your analysis. This helps in gaining targeted insights.

2. **Use Multiple Filters:**

• Combine multiple filters to create more sophisticated criteria. For example, filter responses based on both a specific date range and particular answer choices.

3. **Sort for Clarity:**

• Use sorting to arrange responses in a way that makes the data more readable and facilitates easier analysis. For instance, you can sort responses based on timestamps or numerical values.

4. **Apply to Specific Sheets:**

• If your Google Sheets spreadsheet contains multiple sheets, ensure that you are filtering and sorting on the correct sheet.

5. **Consider Custom Formulas:**

• If your data analysis requires more advanced calculations or conditions, consider using custom formulas in Google Sheets to manipulate and analyze the data further.

6. **Regularly Update Filters:**

- If you're collecting responses over an extended period, regularly update and refine your filters to keep your analysis relevant and up-to-date.

By mastering the filtering and sorting options in Google Sheets, you can efficiently organize and analyze the responses to your Google Form, gaining valuable insights from the collected data.

- **Visualizing Data with Charts**

Visualizing data with charts in Google Sheets adds a layer of clarity and comprehension to your response analysis. Here's a guide on how to create charts based on the responses collected in your Google Form:

1. Access the Google Sheets Spreadsheet:

- If your form is linked to a Google Sheets spreadsheet, click on the "View responses in Sheets" option in the "Responses" tab of the Form Editor.

2. Select Data for Chart:

- Choose the data range you want to visualize. This might involve selecting specific columns or rows that contain the data you want to include in the chart.

3. Open the "Insert" Menu:

- In Google Sheets, go to the "Insert" menu in the toolbar.

4. Choose "Chart":

- Click on "Chart" to open the chart editor.

5. Configure Chart Settings:

- In the chart editor, you can configure various settings, including the chart type, title, and axis labels. Choose the chart type that best suits your data (e.g., bar chart, pie chart, line chart).

6. Customize Chart Appearance:

- Customize the appearance of the chart by adjusting colors, fonts, and other styling options. This helps in making the chart visually appealing and easy to interpret.

7. Preview the Chart:

- As you make changes, preview the chart to see how it will appear. This allows you to fine-tune the settings for optimal visualization.

8. Insert the Chart:

- Once you're satisfied with the chart, click on the "Insert" button to add it to your Google Sheets spreadsheet.

Tips for Visualizing Data with Charts:

1. **Choose Appropriate Chart Types:**

- Select chart types that effectively represent your data. For example, use a bar chart for comparing categories or a line chart for tracking trends over time.

2. Use Color Strategically:

- Incorporate color strategically to highlight important data points or differentiate between categories. Be mindful of color choices to ensure accessibility.

3. Add Titles and Labels:

- Include descriptive titles and labels for your chart to provide context. Clearly label axes and data points to enhance understanding.

4. Explore Different Chart Options:

- Experiment with different chart options to find the most effective visualization for your data. Google Sheets offers various chart types, including scatter plots, histograms, and more.

5. Combine Multiple Charts:

- If your data analysis involves multiple variables or comparisons, consider creating multiple charts and placing them side by side for a comprehensive view.

6. Dynamic Charts with Data Updates:

- If your form is continuously collecting responses, create dynamic charts that automatically update as new data is added. Utilize Google Sheets functions like **OFFSET** or named ranges for dynamic charts.

7. Embed Charts in Presentations or Reports:

- Once you've created charts, you can easily embed them in presentations, reports, or other documents to communicate your findings effectively.

8. Share Charts with Collaborators:

- If you're collaborating with others, share your Google Sheets document to allow collaborators to view and interact with the charts.

By visualizing your data with charts, you can present complex information in a more accessible and understandable format, facilitating better insights and decision-making based on the responses to your Google Form.

- **Exporting Data to Google Sheets**

Exporting data from Google Forms to Google Sheets allows you to conduct more in-depth analysis, create visualizations, and perform various data manipulations. Here's a guide on how to export data to Google Sheets:

1. Access the Google Form:

- Open the Google Form for which you want to export data.

2. Click on the "Responses" Tab:

- In the Form Editor, click on the "Responses" tab at the top.

3. Click on the Google Sheets Icon:

- Click on the Google Sheets icon (a green spreadsheet icon) located in the upper-right corner of the "Responses" tab. This icon represents "Create a new spreadsheet."

4. Choose Destination for the Spreadsheet:

- A prompt will appear asking if you want to create a new spreadsheet or link to an existing one. Choose the desired option based on your preference.

- If you select "Create a new spreadsheet," a new Google Sheets spreadsheet will be created, and the form responses will be automatically linked to it.

- If you select "Select existing spreadsheet," you can choose an existing Google Sheets document to link the form responses to.

5. Access the Linked Spreadsheet:

- Clicking on the Google Sheets icon links the form responses to a spreadsheet. Click on the linked spreadsheet name to open it in Google Sheets.

Tips for Exporting Data to Google Sheets:

1.   **Linking to Existing Sheets:**

•   If you choose to link to an existing spreadsheet, make sure the spreadsheet has the necessary structure to accommodate the form responses. The linked responses will appear as a new sheet within the selected spreadsheet.

2.   **Check Permissions:**

•   Ensure that the Google account you're using has the necessary permissions to create or link to Google Sheets. This is especially important if you're working within an organization.

3.   **Named Ranges for Dynamic Data:**

•   Consider using named ranges in Google Sheets if you plan to create dynamic charts or if you want to reference specific sets of data easily.

4.   **Regularly Update the Linked Sheet:**

•   If your form is actively collecting responses, the linked sheet will update automatically as new responses come in. Regularly check the sheet for the latest data.

5.   **Customize Sheet Layout:**

•   Once the data is in Google Sheets, customize the layout, add additional columns, and perform any necessary data manipulations. This gives you more flexibility for analysis.

6. **Use Google Sheets Features:**

•   Leverage the features of Google Sheets for advanced data analysis, such as sorting, filtering, and creating charts. These tools can help you gain deeper insights from the form responses.

7. **Share Collaboratively:**

•   If you're collaborating with others, share the Google Sheets document to allow collaborators to view and edit the data. Adjust permissions as needed.

By exporting your form data to Google Sheets, you unlock the full potential for analysis and visualization, allowing you to derive meaningful insights and make informed decisions based on the collected responses.

•   **Integrating Forms with Other Google Workspace Apps**

Integrating Google Forms with other Google Workspace apps enhances collaboration, automates workflows, and streamlines data management. Here's a guide on how to integrate Google Forms with other Google Workspace apps:

1. Google Sheets:

•   **Linking Form Responses:**

•   When you collect responses in Google Forms, the data is automatically linked to a Google Sheets spreadsheet. Open the linked spreadsheet to access and manipulate the form responses in Google Sheets.

- **Data Analysis and Visualization:**

- Use Google Sheets to perform in-depth data analysis, create charts, and generate visualizations based on the form responses. The linked spreadsheet updates in real-time as new responses come in.

2. Google Drive:

- **Organizing Form and Responses:**

- Form creators and collaborators can access form files and linked responses directly from Google Drive. The form itself, along with its linked spreadsheet, is stored in Google Drive.

- **Folder Organization:**

- Create folders in Google Drive to organize forms, responses, and related documents. This helps maintain a structured and easily accessible repository.

3. Gmail:

- **Email Notifications:**

- Enable email notifications for new responses directly from the Google Forms "Responses" tab. This keeps form creators informed about new submissions without having to manually check the form.

- **Form Submission Receipts:**

- Use Gmail to send automatic confirmation emails or receipts to respondents upon form submission. This feature is available in the "Responses" tab under the "More options" (three dots).

4. Google Calendar:

- **Event Scheduling:**

- Integrate Google Forms with Google Calendar for event scheduling. Create a form to collect RSVPs or event preferences, and link it to a Google Calendar to manage event details.

- **Automated Calendar Invitations:**

- Use Google Apps Script to automate the creation of calendar events based on form responses. This is especially useful for scheduling appointments or interviews.

5. Google Docs:

- **Document Generation:**

- Create templates in Google Docs and use Google Forms to collect information. Use Google Apps Script to automatically populate these templates with form responses, generating customized documents.

- **Collaborative Editing:**

- Share Google Docs with collaborators and grant them access to view or edit based on their roles. This facilitates collaborative editing of documents linked to form responses.

6. Google Slides:

- **Automated Presentations:**

- Create dynamic presentations in Google Slides based on form responses. Use Google Apps Script to automatically update slides with the latest data from the form.

- **Data Visualization:**

- Embed charts or graphs created in Google Sheets into Google Slides to visually communicate form response data during presentations.

7. Google Sites:

- **Form Embedding:**

- Embed Google Forms directly into Google Sites to gather responses or feedback. This provides a seamless user experience for site visitors.

- **Showcasing Results:**

- Use Google Sites to showcase results, reports, or summaries generated from form responses. This is particularly useful for creating dashboards or informative pages.

Tips for Integration:

1. **Explore Google Apps Script:**

- For advanced automation and customization, explore Google Apps Script. It allows you to create custom functions and triggers to extend the functionality of Google Forms.

2. **Maintain Consistent Naming Conventions:**

- Adopt consistent naming conventions for forms, responses, and related documents in Google Drive. This simplifies navigation and ensures clarity.

3. **Regularly Update and Check Integrations:**

- If you use automated scripts or integrations, regularly check and update them to ensure they align with any changes in your form or workflow.

4. **Train Collaborators:**

• Train collaborators on how to access and use integrated apps. This ensures that everyone involved in the process is familiar with the tools and workflows.

5. **Security Considerations:**

• Be mindful of data security when integrating Google Forms with other apps. Ensure that access permissions are appropriately configured, especially when collaborating with external users.

By integrating Google Forms with other Google Workspace apps, you can create a cohesive and efficient workflow, automating tasks and maximizing the utility of the collected data.

CHAPTER 7
TIPS FOR EFFECTIVE FORMS

- **Crafting Clear and Concise Questions**

Crafting clear and concise questions is essential for gathering accurate and meaningful responses in your Google Form. Here's a guide on how to create questions that are easy to understand:

1. Be Specific and Direct:

- Clearly state the purpose of each question. Avoid vague or ambiguous language that could lead to confusion. Provide specific details to guide respondents in providing the information you need.

2. Use Simple Language:

- Keep your language simple and straightforward. Avoid jargon, technical terms, or complex language that may be unclear to your audience. Aim for a conversational tone that matches the understanding of your target respondents.

3. One Idea Per Question:

- Stick to one idea or concept per question. This helps prevent confusion and ensures that respondents can easily focus on providing a relevant response without being overwhelmed by multiple topics within a single question.

4. Avoid Double-Barreled Questions:

• Double-barreled questions combine multiple ideas or concepts, making it challenging for respondents to provide a clear answer. Split double-barreled questions into separate, more focused questions for accurate responses.

5. Use Closed-Ended Questions for Clarity:

• Closed-ended questions, such as multiple-choice or yes/no questions, are effective for obtaining specific and quantifiable responses. Use these when appropriate to ensure clarity and simplicity.

6. Provide Answer Options:

• When using multiple-choice questions, provide clear and comprehensive answer options. Avoid ambiguous choices and ensure that respondents can easily select the option that best represents their response.

7. Use Likert Scales Judiciously:

• If using Likert scales for rating or agreement, ensure that the scale is consistent and clearly labeled. Clearly define the endpoints (e.g., "Strongly Agree" to "Strongly Disagree") to avoid confusion.

8. Keep Questions Neutral:

- Avoid leading or biased language that could influence respondents' answers. Frame questions in a neutral manner to obtain genuine and unbiased feedback.

9. Test with a Pilot Group:

- Before distributing your form widely, test it with a small pilot group. This allows you to identify any confusing or unclear questions and make adjustments before reaching a larger audience.

10. Seek Feedback:

- If possible, seek feedback from a colleague, friend, or someone from your target audience. They can provide insights into the clarity of your questions and suggest improvements.

11. Use Logical Flow:

- Arrange questions in a logical order that follows a natural flow. Start with simple and non-intrusive questions before moving to more complex or sensitive topics. This helps respondents ease into the survey.

12. Consider Mobile Users:

- If your form will be accessed on mobile devices, ensure that questions are concise and easy to read on smaller screens. Long and complex questions may be challenging for mobile users to navigate.

13. Include Clear Instructions:

- If a question requires specific formatting or details, provide clear instructions. This helps respondents understand how to structure their responses and ensures data consistency.

14. Review and Revise:

- Before finalizing your form, review each question for clarity and conciseness. Revise any language that may be confusing and ensure that the wording aligns with your intended meaning.

By following these guidelines, you can create clear and concise questions in your Google Form, facilitating accurate and meaningful responses from your audience.

- **Maximizing User Engagement**

Maximizing user engagement in your Google Form involves creating an inviting and user-friendly experience. Here's a guide on how to enhance engagement with your form:

1. Craft a Compelling Introduction:

- Begin your form with a clear and engaging introduction. Briefly explain the purpose of the form, why it matters, and how the respondent's input will contribute. A compelling introduction sets a positive tone for engagement.

2. Use a Mix of Question Types:

- Incorporate a variety of question types, including multiple-choice, open-ended, and Likert scale questions. This adds variety and keeps respondents interested throughout the form.

3. Keep the Form Concise:

- Avoid overwhelming respondents with a lengthy form. Keep it concise and focused on gathering essential information. If a question is not crucial, consider whether it can be omitted to streamline the form.

4. Progress Indicators:

- If your form has multiple sections, use progress indicators to show respondents how far they are in completing the form. This provides a sense of accomplishment and encourages them to continue.

5. Mobile-Friendly Design:

- Ensure that your form is mobile-friendly, as many users may access it from their smartphones. Google Forms is designed to be responsive, but testing it on various devices ensures a seamless experience.

6. Appealing Visuals:

- Use visuals sparingly to enhance the aesthetic appeal of your form. This could include images, icons, or even a customized theme. However, ensure that visuals do not distract from the clarity of the questions.

7. Personalize and Contextualize:

- Personalize your form by addressing respondents by name if possible. Provide context for each question so respondents understand why their input is valuable. A personalized and contextualized form feels more relevant to users.

8. Include Skip Logic and Branching:

- Use skip logic and branching to customize the user experience. This ensures that respondents only see questions relevant to their previous answers, preventing them from navigating through irrelevant sections.

9. Offer Clear Navigation:

- Ensure that navigation through the form is intuitive. Include clear buttons for moving forward and backward. Test the navigation to ensure a smooth and frustration-free experience.

10. Immediate Feedback:

- If applicable, provide immediate feedback on responses. This could be in the form of a confirmation message or a summary of their input. Positive reinforcement encourages engagement.

11. Break Long Surveys into Sections:

- For longer surveys, break them into sections with clear titles. This allows respondents to focus on one segment at a time, reducing the perception of the form being too lengthy.

12. Encourage Honesty:

- When asking sensitive or personal questions, assure respondents of the confidentiality of their responses. A safe and non-judgmental environment encourages honest feedback.

13. Social Sharing Options:

- If appropriate, include social sharing options at the end of the form. This allows respondents to share the form with their networks, extending its reach and potentially increasing engagement.

14. Incentives or Rewards:

- Consider offering incentives or rewards for completing the form. This could be a discount, a downloadable resource, or entry into a giveaway. Incentives can significantly boost engagement.

15. Test and Iterate:

- Before launching your form widely, test it with a small group of users and gather feedback. Use this feedback to make improvements and enhance the overall user experience.

By incorporating these strategies, you can create a Google Form that not only collects valuable information but also maximizes user engagement throughout the survey-taking process.

- **Ensuring Accessibility**

Ensuring accessibility in your Google Form is crucial to make it inclusive and usable for a diverse audience. Here's a guide on how to enhance the accessibility of your form:

1. Use Clear and Simple Language:

- Craft questions using clear and simple language. Avoid jargon, complex terminology, or ambiguous phrasing. This ensures that your form is easily understandable by users with varying levels of literacy.

2. Provide Descriptive Instructions:

- Include descriptive instructions for each question. Clearly explain what type of response is expected and any specific formatting requirements. This helps users understand how to interact with the form effectively.

3. Utilize ARIA Attributes:

- Accessible Rich Internet Applications (ARIA) attributes can enhance the accessibility of your form for users with disabilities. Consider using ARIA attributes to provide additional information to screen readers and other assistive technologies.

4. Enable High-Contrast Mode:

- Ensure that your form is readable in high-contrast mode. High-contrast mode is often used by individuals with visual impairments. Test your form's readability by enabling high-contrast mode on your device.

5. Add Alternative Text to Images:

- If your form includes images, charts, or other visual elements, provide alternative text (alt text) that describes the content or purpose of each element. This is essential for users who rely on screen readers.

6. Test with Screen Readers:

- Regularly test your form with screen readers to ensure compatibility. Screen readers provide auditory feedback to users with visual impairments, and optimizing your form for screen readers enhances accessibility.

7. Ensure Keyboard Navigation:

- Confirm that users can navigate through your form using only a keyboard. Some individuals with disabilities may rely on keyboard navigation rather than a mouse. Ensure that all interactive elements are reachable and usable via keyboard input.

8. Optimize Form Structure:

- Organize your form in a logical and sequential manner. Use headings, subheadings, and appropriate formatting to create a clear structure. This helps all users, especially those who rely on screen readers, understand the flow of the form.

9. Test for Color Contrast:

- Check the color contrast of text and background elements to ensure readability for users with visual impairments. Use tools like online color contrast checkers to verify that your form meets accessibility standards.

10. Design for Responsiveness:

- Ensure that your form is responsive and works well on various devices, including smartphones and tablets. Responsive design enhances accessibility by accommodating users who may have different screen sizes and resolutions.

11. Provide Text Alternatives for Multimedia:

- If your form includes multimedia elements such as audio or video, offer text alternatives. This ensures that users who cannot access the multimedia content directly can still understand the information it conveys.

12. Include Closed Captions for Videos:

- If your form includes videos, provide closed captions to make the content accessible to users with hearing impairments. Closed captions also benefit users in environments where audio cannot be played.

13. Test with Real Users:

- Conduct usability testing with individuals who have diverse abilities. Gather feedback from users with disabilities to identify potential accessibility issues and make necessary adjustments.

14. Provide Contact Information for Assistance:

- Include contact information or a help section in your form where users can reach out for assistance with accessibility issues. This demonstrates your commitment to providing support for all users.

15. Stay Informed about Accessibility Standards:

- Stay informed about accessibility standards and guidelines, such as the Web Content Accessibility Guidelines (WCAG).

Regularly check for updates and ensure that your form aligns with the latest best practices in accessibility.

By incorporating these practices, you can create a more inclusive and accessible Google Form, ensuring that all users, regardless of their abilities, can engage with your form effectively.

- **Avoiding Common Pitfalls**

Avoiding common pitfalls is essential to ensure the success and effectiveness of your Google Form. Here's a guide on steering clear of common issues:

1. Overwhelming Length:

- Pitfall: Creating excessively long forms can overwhelm respondents and lead to survey fatigue, affecting the quality of responses.

- Solution: Keep your form concise and focused, only including questions that are necessary for your objectives.

2. Ambiguous Questions:

- Pitfall: Using vague or unclear language in your questions can result in varied and unreliable responses.

- Solution: Craft questions with precision, ensuring that they are easily understandable by your target audience. Avoid double-barreled questions.

3. Lack of Mobile Optimization:

- Pitfall: Neglecting mobile optimization can create a poor user experience for respondents using smartphones or tablets.

- Solution: Test your form on various devices and ensure that it is mobile-friendly. Google Forms is designed to be responsive, but testing is crucial.

4. Limited Accessibility:

- Pitfall: Ignoring accessibility considerations can exclude users with disabilities from engaging with your form.

- Solution: Implement accessibility features such as clear instructions, alternative text for images, and compatibility with screen readers. Test with diverse users.

5. Inadequate Testing:

- Pitfall: Launching a form without thorough testing may result in technical glitches, formatting issues, or unclear instructions.

- Solution: Conduct extensive testing with a variety of users to identify and address any issues. Test on different devices and browsers.

6. Complex Language:

- Pitfall: Using complex language or technical jargon can confuse respondents, leading to inaccurate responses.

- Solution: Choose simple and clear language that aligns with your audience's understanding. Avoid unnecessary complexity in both questions and instructions.

7. Poorly Designed Questions:

- Pitfall: Questions that are poorly designed, overly biased, or leading can skew the results and compromise the integrity of your data.

- Solution: Review each question for neutrality, clarity, and appropriateness. Ensure that response options cover the range of possible answers.

8. Lack of Privacy Assurance:

- Pitfall: Failing to address privacy concerns may deter respondents from providing honest or sensitive information.

- Solution: Clearly communicate the purpose of data collection, assure respondents of data confidentiality, and include a privacy statement if necessary.

9. Insufficient Instructions:

- Pitfall: Providing inadequate or confusing instructions can lead to errors in responses and a negative user experience.

- Solution: Include clear and concise instructions for each question. If necessary, provide examples or guidelines to assist respondents.

10. Ignoring Branding and Theme:

- Pitfall: Neglecting the branding and theme of your form may make it appear unprofessional or untrustworthy.

- Solution: Customize the form's theme, colors, and branding elements to create a visually appealing and cohesive experience for respondents.

11. Ignoring Legal and Ethical Considerations:

- Pitfall: Neglecting legal and ethical considerations, such as obtaining consent for data collection, can lead to legal issues and damage your reputation.

- Solution: Ensure compliance with relevant laws and regulations. Clearly state the purpose of data collection and obtain consent when necessary.

12. Lack of Response Monitoring:

- Pitfall: Failing to monitor responses in real-time may result in missed opportunities for timely follow-ups or interventions.

- Solution: Regularly check response metrics, set up notifications for critical responses, and use features like response validation to ensure data accuracy.

13. Inadequate Communication:

- Pitfall: Poor communication about the form's purpose, expectations, or timeline can result in confusion among respondents.

- Solution: Clearly communicate the purpose of the form, provide context for each question, and set expectations regarding the time required for completion.

14. No Post-Survey Analysis Plan:

- Pitfall: Not having a plan for analyzing and interpreting the collected data may result in valuable insights being overlooked.

- Solution: Develop a post-survey analysis plan, including how you will interpret the data, identify trends, and derive actionable insights.

15. Ignoring User Feedback:

- Pitfall: Neglecting user feedback can prevent you from identifying potential improvements or addressing issues.

- Solution: Encourage users to provide feedback and actively seek insights from respondents. Use feedback to iteratively improve your form for future use.

By avoiding these common pitfalls, you can enhance the effectiveness and user experience of your Google Form, ensuring that it successfully achieves its objectives and provides valuable insights.

- **Staying Updated on New Features**

Staying updated on new features in Google Forms is essential to leverage the latest tools and functionalities for an improved form-building experience. Here are some tips on how to stay informed:

1. Subscribe to Google Workspace Updates:

- Google regularly releases updates and new features across its suite of applications, including Google Forms. Subscribe to the Google Workspace Updates blog to receive notifications about the latest enhancements.

2. Follow Google Workspace Social Media Channels:

- Stay connected with Google Workspace on social media platforms like Twitter, Facebook, and LinkedIn. Google often announces updates and features through these channels.

3. Explore the Google Workspace Help Center:

- Visit the Google Workspace Help Center for comprehensive documentation on Google Forms. The Help Center is regularly updated to include information about new features and best practices.

4. Join Google Workspace Community Forums:

• Participate in the Google Workspace Community forums to engage with other users and Google experts. Discussions often include insights into upcoming features and tips for maximizing the use of existing ones.

5. Check Google Forms Blog and Documentation:

• Google may provide in-depth insights and updates about Google Forms on their official blog. Additionally, explore the Google Forms documentation for detailed information on features and functionalities.

6. Attend Google Workspace Events:

• Keep an eye out for Google Workspace events, webinars, or training sessions. These events often highlight new features and provide demonstrations of how to use them effectively.

7. Enable Google Workspace Updates for Users:

• If you are part of an organization using Google Workspace, ensure that your administrator has enabled the timely rollout of updates. This ensures that users have access to the latest features as soon as they are released.

8. Explore the Early Adopter Programs:

• Google sometimes offers early adopter programs for users interested in testing and providing feedback on upcoming features. Keep an eye out for opportunities to join such programs.

9. Use Google Forms Help Menu:

• Within Google Forms, explore the Help menu for information about updates and new features. Google often includes tips and links to relevant resources directly within the application.

10. Set Up Google Alerts:

• Create Google Alerts for keywords like "Google Forms updates" or "Google Forms new features." This way, you'll receive email notifications whenever there are news articles, blog posts, or announcements related to Google Forms updates.

11. Engage with Google Workspace Beta Programs:

• Google occasionally offers beta programs for users interested in testing upcoming features before the general release. Explore opportunities to join these beta programs and provide feedback.

12. Attend Google Workspace Summits and Conferences:

- Attend Google Workspace summits, conferences, or virtual events where Google often showcases new features and provides insights into the future direction of their applications.

13. Follow Google Forms Product Managers:

- Follow or connect with Google Forms product managers on professional networking platforms like LinkedIn. Product managers often share updates and insights about their products.

14. Check Release Notes:

- Regularly review the release notes provided by Google for Google Forms updates. These notes detail the changes, enhancements, and new features introduced in each release.

By actively exploring these channels and staying engaged with the Google Workspace community, you can ensure that you are informed about the latest features and enhancements in Google Forms, enabling you to make the most of the platform for your form-building needs.

CHAPTER 8

ADVANCED TIPS AND TRICKS

- **Using Add-ons for Enhanced Functionality**

Enhance the functionality of your Google Forms by utilizing add-ons. Here's a guide on how to integrate and leverage add-ons effectively:

1. Explore the Google Workspace Marketplace:

- Visit the Google Workspace Marketplace to explore a variety of add-ons available for Google Forms. This marketplace is a hub for third-party tools that can extend the capabilities of Google Workspace applications.

2. Install Add-ons from the Marketplace:

- Choose relevant add-ons for Google Forms based on your specific needs. Click on the "Install" button for the selected add-on to integrate it with your Google Forms account.

3. Access Add-ons from the Form Editor:

- Once installed, access the add-ons directly from the Google Forms editor. Look for the "Add-ons" menu in the toolbar, where you can find the installed add-ons and explore their functionalities.

4. Popular Google Forms Add-ons:

- Explore popular Google Forms add-ons such as:

- **Form Publisher:** Automates the creation of personalized documents from form responses.

- **Choice Eliminator:** Removes answer choices from multiple-choice questions as they are selected.

- **Form Notifications:** Sends email notifications based on form responses.

- **FormLimiter:** Limits the number of responses, sets a closing date, or disables a form based on specified conditions.

5. Automate Workflows with Add-ons:

- Use add-ons to automate workflows and save time. For example, Form Publisher can automatically generate and email personalized documents, streamlining document creation processes.

6. Collaborate with Team Members:

- If you're working collaboratively, ensure that your team members also have access to and install the necessary add-ons. This ensures a consistent experience and enables collaborative use of add-on features.

7. Stay Updated with Add-on Releases:

- Keep track of updates and new releases for your installed add-ons. Developers often release updates to introduce new features, improve performance, and address any issues.

8. Check Compatibility:

- Before installing an add-on, check its compatibility with the current version of Google Forms. Ensure that the add-on is actively maintained and supported by the developer.

9. Explore FormRanger for Dynamic Choices:

- FormRanger is an add-on that allows you to dynamically update the choices in a multiple-choice, checkbox, or list question based on values from a range of sources such as a spreadsheet or a calendar.

10. Use Advanced Form Approvals:

- Explore add-ons like "Approval Workflow" to add advanced approval processes to your forms. This can be useful for scenarios where responses require review and approval.

11. Experiment with Data Analysis Tools:

- Some add-ons, like "Flubaroo," provide enhanced data analysis features. Experiment with these tools to gain deeper insights into form responses and create more comprehensive reports.

12. Customize Form Appearance with Add-ons:

• Add-ons like "Form Style Editor" allow you to customize the appearance of your Google Form, providing options beyond the default themes available in the form editor.

13. Leverage Google Sheets Add-ons:

• Since Google Forms responses are often linked to Google Sheets, explore Google Sheets add-ons that complement your form data analysis. These can include charting tools, data visualization add-ons, and more.

14. Monitor Add-on Permissions:

• When installing add-ons, be mindful of the permissions they request. Ensure that you are comfortable with the level of access the add-on requires to function properly.

15. Share Add-on Recommendations:

• If you discover a particularly useful add-on, share your recommendations with colleagues or team members. Collaboration on add-on usage can enhance the overall efficiency of your workflow.

By incorporating add-ons into your Google Forms workflow, you can extend the capabilities of the platform, automate processes, and tailor your forms to better suit your specific needs. Regularly explore the Google Workspace Marketplace for new and innovative add-ons that can enhance your form-building and data analysis experiences.

- **Customizing Form URLs**

Customizing the URLs of your Google Forms can add a personalized touch and make it easier for respondents to access your forms. Here's a guide on how to customize form URLs:

1. Create a New Form:

- Start by creating a new form or open an existing one in Google Forms.

2. Click on the Settings Gear:

- In the top-right corner of the form editor, click on the gear icon (Settings).

3. Select "General":

- In the settings menu, select the "General" tab.

4. Click on the "Shorten URL" Option:

- You'll see an option labeled "Shorten URL." Click on it to generate a shortened URL for your form.

5. Customize the Shortened URL:

- Google Forms provides a shortened URL that typically includes random characters. However, you can customize this URL to make it more user-friendly.

6. Enter a Custom Alias:

- After clicking on "Customize," enter a custom alias or keyword that reflects the content or purpose of your form. Note that the alias should be unique and not already in use.

7. Check Availability:

- Google Forms will check the availability of the custom alias. If it's available, you can proceed to save the customized URL.

8. Save the Customized URL:

- Once you've chosen an available custom alias, click "Save." Your form's URL is now customized with the chosen alias.

9. Share the Customized URL:

- You can now share the customized URL with respondents. This URL is more user-friendly and easier to remember than the default URL.

Tips for Customizing Form URLs:

1. Keep it Short and Simple:

- Opt for a short and simple custom alias. Avoid using complex or lengthy words to make the URL easy to remember and share.

2. **Use Keywords:**

•	Incorporate relevant keywords into the custom alias to give respondents an idea of the form's content.

3. **Avoid Special Characters:**

•	Stick to alphanumeric characters and hyphens in your custom alias. Avoid special characters that could cause issues or confusion.

4. **Make it Pronounceable:**

•	If possible, choose a custom alias that is pronounceable. This can make it easier for respondents to share the URL verbally.

5. **Regularly Check Availability:**

•	Custom aliases must be unique. If your preferred alias is already in use, try variations or choose a different alias. Regularly check availability to find a suitable custom alias.

6. **Update Custom URL if Needed:**

•	If your form's content or purpose changes, consider updating the custom alias to reflect the updated information.

7. **Share Customized URLs in Communications:**

- When sharing your form in emails, social media, or other communications, use the customized URL to create a professional and branded appearance.

8. Educate Respondents:

- If you have a specific format for custom aliases, educate respondents on how to access your forms using the customized URL. Provide clear instructions to enhance user experience.

By customizing the URL of your Google Form, you not only create a more user-friendly link but also add a personal touch to your form-sharing process. This customization can be especially beneficial when sharing forms with a broader audience or during marketing and promotional activities.

- **Collaborative Editing and Version History**

Collaborative editing and version history in Google Forms are powerful features that enable multiple users to work together on a form and track changes over time. Here's a guide on how to make the most of these collaborative features:

Collaborative Editing:

1. **Share the Form:**

• Click on the "Send" button in the top-right corner of the form editor to share the form with collaborators. You can invite collaborators via email or generate a shareable link.

2. **Set Permissions:**

• Choose whether collaborators can edit, comment, or only view the form. Adjust permissions based on the level of collaboration you want.

3. **Real-Time Collaboration:**

• Collaborators can edit the form simultaneously in real-time. Changes made by one user are instantly visible to others. Use the comment feature to discuss specific elements of the form.

4. **See Collaborators' Cursors:**

• In the form editor, you'll see the cursors and edits of collaborators in real-time. This visual representation enhances communication and coordination.

5. **Notifications:**

• Google Forms sends notifications when collaborators make changes or add comments. Stay informed about updates to the form.

Version History:

1. **Access Version History:**

• In the form editor, go to "File" and select "Version history." Choose "See version history" to access the version history panel.

2. **View Past Versions:**

• The version history panel shows a timeline of edits. Click on a specific timestamp to view the form as it existed at that point in time.

3. **Restore Previous Versions:**

• To revert to a previous version, click on the timestamp and then select "Restore this version." This is useful if you want to undo changes or compare different versions.

4. **Name Versions:**

• To easily identify versions, use the "Name current version" option in the version history panel. Give each version a descriptive name to signify the changes made.

5. **Automatic Versioning:**

• Google Forms automatically creates versions at significant points, such as when major edits are made or when collaborators save changes. This ensures a comprehensive version history.

Best Practices for Collaboration and Version History:

1. **Communication is Key:**

•   Collaborate effectively by communicating with collaborators through comments or external communication tools. Ensure everyone is on the same page regarding form changes.

2. **Use Comments Wisely:**

•   Utilize the comment feature to leave notes for collaborators. Comments provide context for changes and facilitate discussions about specific elements of the form.

3. **Frequent Saving:**

•   Encourage collaborators to save their work frequently. Google Forms automatically saves changes, but manual saves ensure that the most recent edits are captured in the version history.

4. **Regularly Check Version History:**

•   Periodically check the version history to review changes made to the form. This is especially useful for tracking progress and understanding how the form has evolved over time.

5. **Educate Collaborators:**

•   Ensure that all collaborators are familiar with the collaborative editing and version history features. Provide training if necessary to maximize the benefits of these tools.

6. **Set Clear Permissions:**

• Adjust permissions based on the level of collaboration required. Only provide edit access to users who need to make changes, while others can be given view-only access.

7. **Document Significant Changes:**

• When naming versions, document significant changes or milestones in the form's development. This makes it easier to track the evolution of the form.

8. **Monitor Notifications:**

• Stay informed about changes by monitoring notifications. Notifications alert you to edits and comments made by collaborators.

By leveraging collaborative editing and version history in Google Forms, you can streamline teamwork, track changes effectively, and maintain a comprehensive record of the form's development. These features enhance collaboration and make it easier to manage form creation projects with multiple contributors.

• **Automating Workflows with Google Forms**

Automating workflows with Google Forms can significantly increase efficiency and streamline processes. Here's a guide on how to automate workflows effectively:

1. Integration with Google Workspace:

- Utilize the seamless integration of Google Forms with other Google Workspace applications, such as Google Sheets and Google Drive. Responses can be automatically collected and organized in a connected spreadsheet.

2. Google Forms Add-ons:

- Explore Google Forms add-ons that offer automation features. For example:

- **Form Publisher:** Automatically generates personalized documents based on form responses.

- **Form Notifications:** Sends email notifications when form responses are received.

- **Form Approvals:** Adds approval workflows to form submissions.

3. Google Apps Script:

- Leverage the power of Google Apps Script to create custom automation scripts for your forms. Apps Script allows you to extend the functionality of Google Forms and integrate with other Google Workspace apps.

4. Form Triggers:

- Use triggers in Google Apps Script to set up automated actions based on specific events. For example, you can trigger a script to run when a form is submitted or when specific conditions are met.

5. Auto-populate Fields:

• Pre-fill form fields dynamically by pulling data from external sources using Google Apps Script. This is useful for creating personalized forms based on existing information.

6. Advanced Form Approvals:

• Implement advanced approval processes with Google Apps Script. This can involve sending approval requests to designated users and updating form responses based on the approval status.

7. Google Forms and Google Sheets Integration:

• Automate data transfer between Google Forms and Google Sheets. Responses collected in a Google Sheet can be automatically updated and analyzed without manual intervention.

8. Conditional Logic:

• Implement conditional logic in your form using Google Apps Script. This allows you to show or hide specific form sections based on the user's responses, creating a more dynamic and personalized user experience.

9. Data Validation and Verification:

- Use automation to validate and verify form responses. This can include checking for duplicate entries, ensuring data consistency, and validating responses against predefined criteria.

10. Email Notifications and Alerts:

- Set up automated email notifications or alerts using Google Apps Script. This ensures that key stakeholders are notified in real-time when specific events, such as form submissions, occur.

11. Time-Based Triggers:

- Create time-based triggers to automate actions at scheduled intervals. For example, send reminder emails based on upcoming events or deadlines collected through the form.

12. Integration with External Tools:

- Explore third-party tools and services that integrate with Google Forms. These tools can extend automation capabilities and provide additional features tailored to specific workflows.

13. Multi-step Workflows:

- Design multi-step workflows by combining multiple forms and automation scripts. Each form submission triggers the next step in the workflow, creating a seamless and automated process.

14. Error Handling:

- Implement error handling mechanisms in your automation scripts to address potential issues. This ensures the reliability and resilience of your automated workflows.

15. Regular Monitoring and Maintenance:

- Regularly monitor your automated workflows to ensure they are functioning as intended. Perform routine maintenance and updates to adapt to changing requirements.

By incorporating these automation strategies, you can optimize your workflows, save time, and reduce manual efforts in managing and processing data collected through Google Forms. Whether using built-in features, add-ons, or custom scripts, automation enhances the overall efficiency and effectiveness of your form-based processes.

- **Exploring API Integration for Developers**

For developers looking to integrate Google Forms into their applications or workflows using APIs, there are several options available. Here's a guide on exploring API integration for Google Forms:

1. Google Forms API:

- As of my last knowledge update in January 2022, Google Forms does not have a public API that developers can use directly.

However, Google Workspace APIs, including the Google Sheets API, can be leveraged for certain integration scenarios.

2. Google Sheets API:

- Since Google Forms responses are often stored in Google Sheets, developers can use the Google Sheets API to interact with the spreadsheet that holds form responses. This API allows for reading, writing, and updating data in Google Sheets programmatically.

3. Google Apps Script:

- Google Apps Script provides a scripting platform that allows developers to extend the functionality of Google Workspace applications, including Google Forms. With Google Apps Script, developers can create custom functions, triggers, and automate workflows directly within Google Forms.

4. Scripting with Google Forms:

- In Google Apps Script, developers can write scripts that respond to form submissions, manipulate form data, and trigger actions based on specific events. This scripting capability is a powerful tool for customizing and extending the functionality of Google Forms.

5. Workflow Automation:

• Google Apps Script enables developers to automate workflows, integrate with external APIs, and perform advanced data processing tasks based on form responses. For example, you can automatically send emails, update databases, or trigger other external actions.

6. Google Workspace Add-ons:

• Developers can create and publish Google Workspace add-ons that enhance the functionality of Google Forms. Add-ons can be designed to automate tasks, integrate with external services, and provide additional features within the Google Forms interface.

7. Authentication and Authorization:

• When working with APIs or Google Apps Script, developers need to implement authentication and authorization to ensure secure access to form data. This often involves using OAuth 2.0 for user-based access or service accounts for server-to-server communication.

8. External APIs Integration:

• If your application requires integrating Google Forms data with external APIs, you can use Google Apps Script to make HTTP requests and handle API responses. This allows you to connect Google Forms to a wide range of external services.

9. Regularly Check for Updates:

• Stay informed about updates and new features related to Google Forms API or Google Workspace APIs. Google often releases updates that introduce new capabilities or improvements to existing functionalities.

10. Explore Google Cloud Services:

• For more advanced integration scenarios, developers can explore Google Cloud services. Google Cloud provides a range of services, including Cloud Functions, Cloud Run, and Cloud Pub/Sub, which can be integrated with Google Forms data.

11. Community and Documentation:

• Engage with the developer community and explore documentation to gain insights into best practices and use cases for integrating Google Forms. The Google Apps Script documentation is a valuable resource for developers.

12. Experiment with Code Samples:

• Google provides code samples and examples in the documentation for various scenarios. Experimenting with these samples can help developers understand how to interact with Google Forms programmatically.

Note: Please check the latest documentation and resources for any updates or changes since my last knowledge update in January

2022. Google's APIs and services are subject to updates and improvements.

By exploring these options, developers can enhance the integration capabilities of Google Forms, automate workflows, and create custom solutions tailored to their specific needs.

CONCLUSION

In conclusion, Google Forms is a versatile tool that goes beyond basic surveys, offering a comprehensive platform for creating, sharing, and analyzing online forms. Whether you're a beginner or looking to maximize your proficiency, the step-by-step guide covered key aspects of Google Forms. From the foundational understanding of online forms to advanced features like collaborative editing, version history, automation, and API integration, you've gained insights into the diverse capabilities of this tool.

Remember the power of customization, making your forms not only functional but also visually appealing. User-friendliness is key, and incorporating multimedia elements, logic, and branching can enhance the respondent experience. With the ability to share forms through various channels, including email invitations, website embedding, and QR codes, you have the flexibility to reach your audience effectively.

Analyzing responses in real-time is crucial, and Google Forms offers robust tools for filtering, sorting, visualizing data with charts, and exporting data to Google Sheets. The guide also emphasized the importance of clear and concise question crafting, maximizing user engagement, ensuring accessibility, and avoiding common pitfalls in form creation.

For developers, the guide introduced the concept of API integration using Google Apps Script and other Google Workspace APIs, showcasing the potential for customizing and automating workflows to meet specific requirements.

As you navigate the world of Google Forms, staying updated on new features, leveraging add-ons for enhanced functionality, and embracing collaborative editing and version history are key strategies for continuous improvement. By following these guidelines and tips, you're well-equipped to harness the full potential of Google Forms for your surveys, feedback collection, data analysis, and beyond. Happy form creating!

www.ingramcontent.com/pod-product-compliance
Lightning Source LLC
Chambersburg PA
CBHW070526160726
48003CB00004B/1710